The Countryside

LIFE IN ELIZABETHAN ENGLAND

The Countryside

KATHRYN HINDS

MARSHALL CAVENDISH BENCHMARK   NEW YORK

To Jack and Marilyn

The author and publisher specially wish to thank Dr. Megan Lynn Isaac,
former associate professor of Renaissance Literature at Youngstown State University, Ohio,
for her invaluable help in reviewing the manuscript

MARSHALL CAVENDISH BENCHMARK 99 WHITE PLAINS ROAD TARRYTOWN, NEW YORK 10591-9001
www.marshallcavendish.us Text copyright © 2008 by Marshall Cavendish Corporation All rights reserved. No part of
this book may be reproduced or utilized in any form or by any means electronic or mechanical including photocopying,
recording, or by any information storage and retrieval system, without permission from the copyright holders. All Internet
sites were available and accurate when this book was sent to press. LIBRARY OF CONGRESS CATALOGING-IN-PUBLICATION
DATA Hinds, Kathryn, 1962- The Countryside / by Kathryn Hinds p. cm. — (Life in Elizabethan England) Summary:
"A social history of Elizabethan England, focusing on life on the farms and in the villages of rural England during the
reign (1558–1603) of the famous monarch"—Provided by publisher. Includes bibliographical references and index.
ISBN 978-0-7614-2543-4 1. England--Social life and customs--16th century--Juvenile literature. 2. Country life--
England--History--16th century--Juvenile literature. 3. Farm life--England--History--16th century--Juvenile literature.
4. Great Britain--History--Elizabeth, 1558–1603--Juvenile literature. I. Title. DA320.H56 2007 307.720942'09031--
dc22 2007013185

EDITOR: Joyce Stanton   PUBLISHER: Michelle Bisson
ART DIRECTOR: Anahid Hamparian   SERIES DESIGNER: Michael Nelson

Images provided by Rose Corbett Gordon, Art Editor, Mystic CT, from the following sources:
Cover: Bettmann/Corbis   Back cover: Victoria & Albert Museum, London/Art Resource, NY   Pages 1,2-
3,14,30,34,39,41,42,44,56,57,60,65,68: The Granger Collection, NY; page 6: Historical Picture Archive/Corbis; page 8:
Private Collection, Photo © Christie's Images/Bridgeman Art Library; page 11: The Art Archive/Bodleian Library Oxford;
page 12: Topham/The Image Works; page 16: Private Collection, © Chris Beetles, London/Bridgeman Art Library; page
17: British Library, London/Bridgeman Art Library; page 18: Rafael Valls Gallery, London/Bridgeman Art Library; page
21: ARPL/Topham/The Image Works; page 22: ©Anna Stowe; pages 24,29,36,66 left & right: Victoria & Albert Museum,
London/Art Resource, NY; page 25: Gwydir Castle, Gwynedd, Wales/Bridgeman Art Library; page 26: Pierpont Morgan
Library/Art Resource, NY; page 33: Stapleton Collection/Corbis; pages 40, 54-55: British Library Board. All Rights
Reserved/Bridgeman Art Library; pages 47,62: Tate Gallery, London/Art Resource, NY; page 49: Hardwick Hall,
Derbyshire, UK, National Trust Photographic Library/John Hammond/Bridgeman Art Library; page 50: The Berger
Collection at the Denver Art Museum/Bridgeman Art Library; page 52: Hatfield House, Hertfordshire, UK/The
Bridgeman Art Library; page 59: Christie's Images/SuperStock; page 70: Private Collection/Bridgeman Art Library.

Printed in Malaysia
135642

front cover: A farm family works together to harvest wheat, in a painting made in the 1500s by an unidentified artist.
half-title page: Marigolds like these, from a 1597 book about herbs, grew in many Elizabethan gardens.
title page: A shepherd with his flock and trusty sheepdog, painted by Pieter Brueghel the Elder around 1555.
back cover: This stained-glass window depicts a man planting grain.

CONTENTS

A country gentleman of the early 1600s dozes beside a comfortable fire in his parlor.

About Elizabethan England

IT WAS A GOLDEN AGE: A TIME OF POETRY, THEATER, AND SONG; intrigue, adventure, and exploration; faith, intellect, and passion; trials, triumphs, and splendor. The reign of Elizabeth I, from 1558 to 1603, was like no other era of English history. Under Elizabeth's leadership, England began the journey from small, isolated, poor island nation to thriving world power. Under the poets and playwrights of Elizabeth's time—above all, William Shakespeare—the English language reached new heights, and a powerful body of literature was created, one that still delights and inspires us. Elizabeth invited and influenced other forms of creativity as well, and her rule left indelible marks not only in the arts but in politics, religion, and society. The glories—and the troubles—of her reign are all part of the heritage shared by England and its former colonies.

This series of books looks at the Elizabethan age with a focus on its people and their everyday lives, whether they were at the top of society, the bottom, or somewhere in the middle. We will see how they worked, where they lived, how they related to one another, how they relaxed and celebrated special occasions, how they coped with life's hardships. In this volume we will meet the people of the English countryside: farmers and shepherds, country gentlemen, housewives, and more. These people had many of the same joys and sorrows, hopes and fears that we do. They were poised at the beginning of the modern age, but still their world was very different from ours. Forget about telephones, computers, cars, and televisions, and step back in time. . . . Welcome to life in Elizabethan England!

Country Communities

There fruitful corn, fair trees, fresh herbage is
And all things else that living creatures need.
— EDMUND SPENSER, *COLIN CLOUTS COME HOME AGAINE*

"THIS LAND OF SUCH DEAR SOULS, THIS DEAR DEAR land": so Shakespeare referred to England in his play *Richard II*. At the time he was writing, the late 1500s, there were probably around 4 million "dear souls" in England. Nearly all of them lived and worked in rural areas, and even city dwellers depended on the labor and products of the countryside for food, raw materials, and much of their income.

England was a fertile country, rich in resources. Most areas were supplied with plentiful water, from rivers, streams, and natural springs. The terrain included seacoasts, river valleys, mountains, rolling hills, and level, open lands. There were marshes, moors, meadows, and forests. All this variety offered a wide range of opportunities for fishing, hunting, mining, and of course raising crops and livestock.

Opposite: The Avon River, looking toward William Shakespeare's birthplace, the market town of Stratford-upon-Avon. The steeple belongs to Holy Trinity Church, where Shakespeare was both baptized and buried.

Most of the country's agricultural products were used by the English themselves, but one rural commodity was widely exported and essential to the nation's economy: wool. Even in areas that could not grow many crops, sheep could still graze. English wool was highly valued all over Europe, and German traveler Paul Hentzner made a point of writing about it when he visited England in 1598:

> There are many hills without one tree, or any spring, which produce a very short and tender grass, and supply plenty of food to sheep; upon these wander numerous flocks, extremely white, and whether from the temperature of the air, or goodness of the earth, bearing softer and finer fleeces than those of any other country: this is the true Golden Fleece, in which consist the chief riches of the inhabitants, great sums of money being brought into the island by merchants, chiefly for that article of trade.

FIELDS, VILLAGES, AND MARKET TOWNS

In much of England, especially during the earlier part of Elizabeth's reign, farming was organized the same way it had been for hundreds of years. The system was known as champion, champaign, or open-field agriculture, referring to the large fields surrounding a typical farming community. The number of fields varied from two or three up to eight or more. Every field was divided into strips, and every farm family had strips of land in each field. Farmers therefore worked the fields as a community, deciding together what to plant in each and which to leave fallow for the season or year, and jointly organizing plowing, sowing, and harvesting times.

In addition to the fields, the community shared pastures, mead-

ows, and woodlands. Everyone's livestock grazed in the common pastures, while the meadows grew long grass that would be cut for hay. The woods provided firewood, materials for making and mending tools and furniture, acorns and beechnuts for pigs to eat, and habitat for deer and other game animals. Also, a common area often supplied the community with gravel, sand, stone, and similar resources.

Open-field farming was not suitable for some regions, such as places that were very hilly or heavily wooded. And during the course of Elizabeth's reign, champion agriculture gave way more and more to farming "in several." This is the type of farming we are most familiar with, in which a single family works its own fields, separate from those of the neighbors—although the Elizabethans often continued to share pastures and meadows. But individual families' croplands and pastures were likely to be enclosed by hedges or stone walls. Many people found that farming in several produced

This seventeenth-century map shows some of the woodlands, pastures, and strips of farmland that surrounded the village of Laxton. In the northern county of Nottinghamshire, Laxton is the only place in England where open-field farming is still practiced.

higher yields and therefore higher profits. Farmer-poet Thomas Tusser, for example, declared, "Good land that is several, crops may have three, / in champion country it may not so be."

Whether the land was worked in common or in several could determine much about how rural people lived, including where they lived. In his 1587 *Description of England,* William Harrison explained,

> Our soil being divided into champion ground and woodland, the houses of the first lie uniformly builded in every town together, with streets and lanes; whereas in the woodland countries (except here and there in great market towns) they stand scattered abroad, each one dwelling in the midst of his own occupying.

As this passage indicates, there were three main types of rural settlement. One, typical of open-field country, was the village, surrounded by its fields and other common lands. Then there were more-or-less isolated farmhouses, each surrounded by the lands worked by just one family, with the fields separated by hedges or woods. Finally, there were market towns, located an easy distance from a number of villages or farms so that farmers could go to town to sell their produce and buy items that they could not make or grow themselves. The market towns were generally bounded by agricultural land, which many of the townspeople worked. Other townspeople, though, made their living at crafts or trades, such as hat making, blacksmithing, or buying and selling wool.

Perhaps the most famous of all Elizabethan market towns is Stratford-upon-Avon, the birthplace of William Shakespeare, whose father was a glove maker, wool trader, landowner, and moneylender. Stratford had a population of about two thousand, a market day once a week, a grammar school, orchards and gardens, and, only a short walk away, fields, farms, and woods. One nearby area was the Forest of Arden, which had once been a great, unbroken expanse of trees. By Shakespeare's time, many parts of the forest had been enclosed, so Arden was broken up into woodland and pasture. Shakespeare created an imaginary version of the Forest of Arden as the setting of his 1599 play *As You Like It*, where shepherds' cottages and fields fringed a deep, mysterious wood.

RURAL SOCIETY

Stratford-upon-Avon was a free, self-governing town, as were many others. But numerous towns, villages, and farmsteads were parts of manors, estates that were the property of wealthy landowners, often noblemen. Some of these landowners had many estates, which could be in different parts of the country. They might rarely visit each of their holdings, which would be run for them by stewards

A Shakespearean Shepherd's Life

In Shakespeare's play *As You Like It*, a group
of nobles are living in exile in the Forest of
Arden. One of the exiles has been accompa-
nied by a fool, or court jester, named
Touchstone. In this scene Touchstone and
the shepherd Corin, who lives on the edge
of the forest, compare their opinions about
rural life.

Shepherds shear sheep while the farm's owner
looks on.

CORIN   And how like you this shepherd's life,
          Master Touchstone?

TOUCHSTONE   Truly, shepherd, in respect of
     itself, it is a good life; but in respect that it is a shepherd's life, it is naught. In respect that it
     is solitary, I like it very well; but in respect that it is private, it is a very vile life. Now in
     respect that it is in the fields, it pleaseth me well; but in respect it is not in the court, it is
     tedious. As it is a spare life, look you, it fits my humour well; but as there is no more plenty
     in it, it goes much against my stomach. Hast any philosophy in thee, shepherd?

CORIN   No more but that I know the more one sickens, the worse at ease he is, and that he
     that wants money, means, and content is without three good friends; that the property of rain
     is to wet, and fire to burn; that good pasture makes fat sheep; and that a great cause of the
     night is lack of the sun; that he that hath learned no wit by nature nor art may complain of
     good breeding or comes of a very dull kindred.

TOUCHSTONE   Such a one is a natural philosopher. Wast ever in court, shepherd?

CORIN   No, truly.

TOUCHSTONE   . . . Why, if thou never wast at court thou never sawest good manners. . . .

CORIN   Not a whit, Touchstone. Those that are good manners at the court are as ridiculous in
     the country as the behavior of the country is most mockable at the court. . . . I am a true
     labourer. I earn that [that which] I eat, get [make] that [that which] I wear; owe no man hate,
     envy no man's happiness; glad of other men's good, content with my harm; and the greatest
     of my pride is to see my ewes graze and my lambs suck [nurse].

and other officials. Generally, one estate would be the main residence, with a splendid home set in its own grounds. Other landowners had only one manor, and its grounds might be just another section of the village. Many landowners, though, spent much of their time in London, the capital.

The greatest landowners were the nobles—the barons, viscounts, earls, marquises, and dukes, whose families had often held land and title for generations. Noblemen were sometimes referred to as "gentlemen of the greater sort," while "gentlemen of the lesser sort" were the gentry, nonnoble landowners who were still wealthy enough that they didn't have to do any physical work on the land themselves. England had only fifty-seven noblemen when Elizabeth came to the throne; during her reign she granted noble rank to just a few more in reward for their service. The gentry were more numerous, and their numbers increased when city craftsmen and tradesmen made enough money—as they sometimes did—to buy land and stop working.

Nobles and gentry together made up a very small proportion of England's population—perhaps as little as 2 percent. Their influence, on the other hand, was great. Even citizens of a self-governing town or village often sought guidance and assistance from the leading gentleman of the area, and treated him with great respect. And it was country gentlemen who served as justices of the peace, the national government's official representatives on the local level. Chosen by a royal commission, justices of the peace were responsible for judging legal cases, enforcing laws, implementing the decisions of the queen and her council, organizing the maintenance of bridges and roads, and similar matters.

For all the gentlemen's prestige, in many ways the most important class was that of yeoman farmers, those who owned all or a

A prosperous family relaxes together in their well-appointed country home, in an Elizabethan scene imagined by a nineteenth-century artist

good portion of the land they worked. Yeomen were the backbone of rural society—of English society as a whole, according to many Elizabethan writers. William Harrison expressed their role this way:

> Yeomen are those which . . . [are] freemen born English. . . . This sort of people have a certain pre-eminence, and more estimation than labourers and artificers [craftspeople], and commonly live wealthily, keep good houses and travel to get riches. They are also for the most part farmers to gentlemen, and with grazing, frequenting of markets and keeping of servants (not idle servants as the gentlemen do, but such as get both their own and part of their masters' living) do come to great wealth, insomuch that many of them are able and do buy the lands of unthrifty gentlemen, and often setting their sons to the schools . . . or otherwise leaving them sufficient lands whereupon they might live without labour, do make them by those means to become gentlemen.

Surveyors mark off the boundaries of a yeoman's land, from a book printed around 1590.

As Harrison indicated, the line between prosperous yeomen and gentlemen "of the lesser sort" could be a thin one. If a yeoman or his son did acquire enough land and wealth to rise to the gentry, he would hire laborers to work some of his land, raising the crops he and his family needed. The rest of his holdings could be rented out to tenant farmers. These husbandmen, as they were sometimes called, typically worked twenty to thirty acres, enough (in a good year) to feed their families and pay the rent. Many country dwellers, though, were cottagers, called this because all they owned (or rented) was a cottage and an acre or two of ground. This was not enough to support a family, so in addition to growing what they could, cottagers usually hired themselves out as farm laborers. Some, though, might have a craft or trade that they could work, and could get by on that.

ANNO 1602.

ECCE SIC BENEDICETVR HOMO.
QVI TIMET DOMINVM.

Home Sweet Home

Thy houses and barns would be looked upon:
and all thing amended . . . [before] harvest come on.
Things thus set in order, at quiet and rest:
thy harvest goeth forward and prospereth best.
— Thomas Tusser, *A hundreth good pointes of husbandrie*

ELIZABETHAN HOUSEHOLDS WERE GENERALLY LARGER than ours. A typical rural family consisted of husband, wife, and, on average, three to five children. Occasionally there might be one or two grandparents living in the home, too. Most people, however, did not live long enough to need the younger generation to take care of them—death before the age of forty was all too common. But although elderly relatives were unusual in the home, household servants were not. All but the poorest English families had at least one or two servants who lived with the family. In rural areas, servants could include farm laborers, although many such hired hands lived in their own cottages. And if the father of the family practiced a skilled craft, such as blacksmithing, he would usually have at least one apprentice, who would also live in the home. Not surprisingly, then, most Elizabethan households were fairly crowded, and privacy was a rare luxury.

Opposite: Gathered around their dining table, a family says grace before eating. The Latin words at the bottom translate, "Behold how a man is blessed who fears the Lord."

19

Rural Housing

Most houses in rural England, wrote William Harrison,

> have neither dairy, stable, nor brewhouse annexed unto them under the same roof (as in many places beyond the sea and some of the north parts of our country) but all separate from the first and one of them from another. And yet for all this they are not so far distant in sunder but that the goodman lying in his bed may lightly hear what is done in each of them with ease and call quickly unto his meinie [household] if any danger should attach [seize] him.

We begin to get a picture of a well-off yeoman's farm. There is the house where the family and servants live, then there are a number of outbuildings. Harrison mentions three—one for processing dairy products, one for sheltering horses, and one for brewing ale (the everyday drink of most English people). There may be others, which could include a barn for storing grains and hay; sheds and enclosures for cows, chickens, and pigs; and a workshop where tools could be made and repaired. Many of these buildings would likely be arranged around three sides of a rectangular farmyard, an area providing work space for tasks ranging from slaughtering livestock to making soap or dying cloth.

In most places, houses and farm buildings were primarily of wood. Timber-framed construction was common: the main structural supports were thick oak beams, and the places between them were filled with wattle and daub, woven sticks plastered with a mix of mud and straw. Wealthier people might use brick instead of wattle and daub as fill, but building a whole house out of brick was rare at this time. Stone was a favored house-building material in areas

How Does Your Garden Grow?

SILIQVASTRVM
TERTIVM.

Langer Indianischer Pfeffer.

733

qq

A new food plant from the Americas: cayenne peppers, shown in a sixteenth-century illustration

"Flowers to smell, roots to eat, herbs for the pot"—so poet Richard Barnfield summed up the basic requirements of a garden. Almost every rural family would have at least one, close to the house—a kitchen garden to supply vegetables, herbs, and some fruits. It was usually tended by the housewife. Among the things she could grow were asparagus, carrots, cucumbers, lettuces, onions, radishes, spinach, and strawberries. She cultivated many herbs, including lavender, marjoram, mint, parsley, rosemary, sage, savory, thyme, and wormwood. She used these plants in food, medicines, and various household preparations. For example, herbs such as rosemary, lavender, and wormwood were strewn on the floor or used in other ways to help repel fleas and other problem insects. Similarly, the flowers in the garden had a variety of purposes. Some, like violets and marigolds, could be used to flavor and color food. Roses and lavender were often distilled to make fragrant water for cooking, hand washing, and scenting linens. But many flowers were enjoyed just for their beauty. In addition to the flowers already mentioned, the Elizabethans loved lilies, daisies, hyacinths, carnations, primroses, columbines, daffodils (which they often called daffadillies), and many others.

These slate-roofed stone cottages in a market town were built around 1380 as storehouses for wool and were later converted into homes and workshops for weavers.

where it was easy to get, but otherwise it was expensive and only used by the wealthy. In some places, cob walls were not unusual. They were made from a mix of clay, straw, stones, and water, then plastered or whitewashed. This was a more durable material than it sounds—there are Elizabethan cob-walled houses still standing today.

Roofs were most commonly thatched with straw or reeds. Thatch was great for insulation but also provided a cozy environment for rodents and insects. In damp areas, the thatch may have needed replacing almost every year (but the rotting thatch made good compost to help fertilize fields or gardens). Roofs could also be covered with clay tiles, wooden shingles, or slate, depending on how available the raw materials were locally or how well-off the house owner was. Window coverings also depended on wealth. People who could not afford glass windows might have to make do with just a sheet of oiled linen to keep out cold and insects but still let in light. Harrison tells us that "of old time our country houses in stead of glass did use much lattice"—screens woven of willow branches or strips of oak—or even panels of horn fixed into wooden frames. "But as horn in windows is now quite laid down in every place, so our lattices are also grown into less use, because glass is come to be so plentiful."

Most country dwellings were quite small, with a single story and as few as two rooms. The front room, often called the hall, was a combination of kitchen, dining room, workroom, and family room. The other room was a bedchamber for the parents and young children of the family; older children, servants, and other household members would usually sleep in the hall, or perhaps in a loft above it. The more well-off a family was, the more rooms their home was likely to have, and it might have two stories instead of only one. Additional rooms could include a kitchen separate from the hall, a pantry, a buttery (where liquids were kept), and another bedroom or two.

COTTAGE COMFORTS (AND DISCOMFORTS)

There was one room, which we take for granted, that almost no Elizabethan house had: a bathroom. At home, people used either chamber pots or outdoor latrines. In the fields, they just relieved themselves behind a bush or hedge, if they bothered to screen themselves at all—Elizabethans often did not expect much privacy in such matters. Standards of personal cleanliness were different, too, since there was no indoor plumbing. A hot bath involved hauling and heating a lot of water, so most people made do with just washing their face and hands every day in a washbasin. Nearly every village, though, had a stream or pond or other body of water in which people could bathe if they wanted to—at least when the weather was warm.

Staying warm in winter could be a challenge, since there was no way to distribute heat evenly to every part of a house. Some homes were still heated in the medieval style, with an open hearth in the center of the hall. In this case, there was no chimney, so smoke just drifted up and hung in the air, only some of it eventually seeping out through a hole in the roof. More and more

Cooking in an iron cauldron hung over an old-fashioned open hearth

houses, though, had at least one fireplace, with a brick or wattle-and-daub chimney to funnel the smoke to the outside. People burned wood, coal, or (in some northern and moorland areas) peat, and staying well supplied with fuel was a constant chore.

The fire was where all cooking was done, and it was also the main source of light. Other indoor lighting could come from candles, oil lamps, or rushlights. But candles were expensive (beeswax candles even more so than tallow), and none of these light sources could illuminate more than their immediate area; a rushlight barely even did that much. So most of the time, country people went to bed when the sun went down and got up before sunrise so that they could make the most of every minute of daylight.

Most rural homes did not have much furniture. Nor did the average family have space for much, since a lot of room was taken up by equipment: a spinning wheel, a butter churn, buckets, baskets and barrels, and so on. Country people did not usually own many clothes—sometimes only two different outfits—so an entire family's wardrobe might be stored in just a few wooden chests. Other chests stored tablecloths and napkins, spoons and knives (forks were very rare in England at this time), cups, and dishes (wooden for poorer people, pewter for the better-off). A prosperous yeoman family might have enough tableware, and of good quality, that they would own a cupboard that could both store and display it.

The Countryside

Most people would have a rectangular oak table for working and eating at. Seating could include wooden benches, stools, and chairs, as well as the storage chests and overturned buckets if needed. Many families owned only one chair, which was normally used by the father. The parents generally had a big wooden bed, surrounded by curtains to hold in heat and provide a little privacy. Small children might sleep in a trundle bed that slid out from under the big bed. Some people just slept on mattresses on the floor. The best mattresses were stuffed with feathers; others were filled with wool or, the least expensive option, with straw or chaff.

A wealthy family's elaborately carved oak bed, made in Wales in 1570

Elizabeth's reign was a time of increasing prosperity for the English middle classes—the "middling sort," as yeoman farmers and their city counterparts, merchants and master craftsmen, were often called. By the end of the sixteenth century, it was possible for these people to enjoy some of the same comforts and luxuries as the gentry, leading William Harrison to write,

> Many farmers . . . have for the most part learned also to garnish their cupboards with plate, their joined beds with tapestry and silk hangings, and their tables with carpets and fine napery, whereby the wealth of our country (God be praised therefore, and give us grace to employ it well) doth infinitely appear.

Men of the Soil

A man may behold the fields round about . . .
with such comfortable abundance of all kind of grain,
that the husbandman which waiteth for the fruits of his labours
cannot but clap his hands for joy.
—JOHN NORDEN, *SPECULUM BRITANNIAE*

MOST WORK IN THE ELIZABETHAN COUNTRYSIDE WAS
based in or near the home. Only a few occupations—mining and
shipbuilding, for example—required a man to commute to his
job. Even then, he probably didn't have a very long walk to work.
In general, though, rural men spent their days in fields and pastures, raising crops and livestock. Some farmers produced all or
nearly all of the grain, wool, meat, and so on that their families
consumed. But most farm families were not so self-sufficient.
They might raise some of what they needed, but most of the
agricultural goods they produced were intended for sale. With
the money earned from selling wheat or milk or wool or fruit,
farmers could then buy a variety of necessaries, and maybe even
some luxuries.

Opposite: The grain harvest usually began in
August, ushering in one
of the busiest seasons of
a farmer's year.

WORKING THE LAND

The most important crops were grains: wheat, rye, oats, and barley. These were the basic ingredients for bread, porridge, and ale, all staples of the English diet. In addition, oats were fed to horses and other farm animals. Other staples were peas and beans. During Elizabeth's reign, farmers also cultivated specialized crops: flax, for linen; hemp, for rope and cloth; madder, for red dye; and woad, for blue dye. In some areas, farmers planted large areas with hops, used in brewing beer. Elsewhere, orchards were important—favorite fruits were cherries and apples. Near London, farmers had large market gardens where they raised fruits and vegetables to sell to the inhabitants of the great city.

In some parts of England the land and climate were unsuitable for growing grain, so rural people focused on herding sheep or cattle. Sheep were especially adaptable, able to graze even on inhospitable moorlands. Elsewhere, though, raising crops and raising livestock went hand in hand. Farmers needed oxen or horses to pull their plows, and these animals needed pastures. Where there were pastures, it only made sense to graze cows and sheep as well. Both could provide milk, meat, and leather, and sheep of course were the source of wool. And when all the crops had been harvested from a field, the animals could graze on the stalks and straw that remained—in the process, leaving behind manure to fertilize the field.

Caring for crops and livestock was hard physical work, and farmers put in long days, their labors varying through the seasons. The agricultural year began in September with planting the crops that would grow over the winter. Farmers typically sowed rye in September and wheat in October. Then they had to weed around the young plants, clean out drainage ditches, and trim hedges.

Autumn was also the time to harvest fruit and nuts and to herd pigs into the woods to eat acorns and beechnuts.

As the weather got colder in November, the farmer brought his livestock in from the pastures. Horses would be stabled over the winter, as would dairy cows and some other animals, so that they could breed in the spring. But much of the stock would be slaughtered and the meat salted or smoked to preserve it. This way the farmer did not have too many animals to feed through the winter, and he and his family would have meat to eat during the cold months. Another chore for this time of year was cleaning the outhouse and spreading the muck in the garden to fertilize it.

A farmer sows seeds for winter wheat in October.

Not much outdoor work was done in December and January, and Christmas brought a season of relaxation and festivity. But there was still plenty to do. Tools had to be repaired, seeds had to be sorted, the livestock had to be fed and their stables cleaned. This was also a good time to make baskets and other things needed around the house and farm. And now when heating was especially important, there was always wood to chop for the fire.

As January ended, agriculture got under way again. As soon as the ground was soft enough, manure was spread on the fields and plowing began. In some areas, oats could be planted before this month was ended. Spring began in February, when peas and beans were sown and animals started to mate. Another February task was to look in the hedges and woods, before the leaves came out, for wood that could be made into farm tools. As Thomas Tusser recommended:

Thy servant in walking thy pastures about:
for yokes, [hay]forks and rakes, let him look to find out.
And after at leisure, let this be his hire:*　　　　[*job, task]
to trim them and make them, at home by the fire.

A boy goads the oxen while his father guides the plow, readying a field for planting. This illustration comes from the first English book on agriculture, printed in 1523.

In March the farmer planted his barley and might sow grass seed in his pastureland. This was also the time to plant hops and to start preparing the garden. By early April, planting the garden was well under way. And all through the spring months there were the young crops to care for and animals to look after. There were no veterinarians in Elizabethan England, so if livestock were hurt or ill, the farmer had to do his best to doctor them himself. By the end of April, the animals could graze in the pastures again.

Summer began in May. There was plenty of weeding to do in the fields, and many farmers now plowed the fields they planned to sow in the fall. May was also a good month for tending to wooded areas, cutting or planting trees as necessary. But there was also time to enjoy the mild weather and the blooming flowers. In June, though, country people got very busy again. The first part of the month was devoted to sheepshearing and preparing the wool for sale or storage. Then it was time to get out to the meadows and mow the long grass. There were no machines to help with this: Elizabethans cut their grass with an iron-bladed scythe.

The cut grass was spread out to dry and was tended through July. It had to be checked and turned frequently to make sure it was not rotting. The thoroughly dry grass, or hay, was stacked and loaded into carts to be stored in the barn for the winter, when the cows and horses would feed on it. More plowing was done in July, too, and peas and beans were ready for harvest.

In August it was time to begin harvesting the grain, a long and painstaking process. Day after day, farmworkers walked along the rows of rye, wheat, barley, and oats, swinging their sickles to cut the stalks of grain, a handful at a time. Other workers followed behind to gather the stalks, bind them into sheaves, and load them into carts to be transported to the barn. Harvesting could only be done when the weather was dry because wet grain would quickly spoil. On rainy days, farmers and laborers threshed the grain by beating it with a wooden tool to break open the grain husks. Then the grain was winnowed. This was often done by waving straw fans over the threshed grain; the breeze created would blow away the husks and straw, leaving the nutritious seeds to be gathered up and stored or sold. The threshing and winnowing went on throughout September, and then it was time to begin the whole agricultural cycle again.

MORE WAYS TO MAKE A LIVING

Few farmers worked their land all by themselves. Naturally family members and servants participated in the agricultural routine. In addition, any farmer who could afford to would hire temporary laborers for haymaking, harvest, and other especially busy times. There were always people looking for this employment. A large portion of farmworkers and other rural laborers had little, if any, land and so needed to work for others. The shepherd Corin in Shakespeare's *As You Like It* is in just that situation: "I am shepherd to another man, / And do not shear the fleeces that I graze." In other words, he did the work of herding and raising the sheep, but it was his employer who got the profits from their wool.

Many farmers did a substantial business buying and selling agricultural products, especially meat, wool, and leather. Some sold timber and other forest products. Others were involved in manufacturing: in addition to farming, they might produce such goods as clay pots, nails, or knitted stockings. A number of well-off farmers also ran mills, mines, forges, or iron furnaces on their property.

Mining was becoming a more and more important part of the English economy and employed an increasing number of people in the countryside. Lead, tin, copper, and iron were the principle metals found in England, and all were profitable to mine. So, too, was coal, which was in growing demand for fueling the furnaces used by glassmakers and brickmakers. It was being used in home heating as well.

Another important mineral resource was salt, which was produced in coastal areas by letting sea water fill depressions in the ground and then evaporate. Rural people living near rivers or the ocean could also make at least part of their living from fishing or, if they had the skills, boatbuilding. Fishing was an important means of livelihood for the inhabitants of marshlands. They also harvested reeds and other useful water plants and raised many sheep, cattle, and horses. In addition they caught waterfowl, fattened them up, and then sold them to city markets, where wealthy gourmets would buy them.

Miners at work, preparing metal ore for transport to market

Transportation by water could be much quicker and easier than transportation by land, so some rural men ran ferries or took cargo on barges or crewed ships. Many sailors, such as the famous Sir Francis Drake, who sailed around the world, were from country villages, especially in the south and southwest. England was becoming a great seafaring nation, with numerous far-traveling merchant ships. Sometimes, though, the captains were so eager for profit that they might start preying on other ships. Often the captured ships belonged to an enemy nation, especially Spain, and in that case the English captains could be considered patriotic privateers. But it might not look that way outside England, whose seamen became rather notorious; as Paul Hentzner wrote, "they are good sailors, and better pirates."

Diary of a Country Gentleman

For about a year in the mid-1570s, a country gentleman named William Carnsew kept a daily record of his activities. Carnsew lived in Cornwall, in southwest England, where he owned property in several villages. Most of his land was farmed, but he had mines on some of it. In his diary we see him acting as a justice of the peace, worrying about his family and friends, commenting on gossip and current events, making note of the books he was reading, ordering supplies for his farms, overseeing planting and harvesting, and going out in all kinds of weather to visit his holdings. Here is a selection from his entries for August, starting on the first of the month:

Sir Thomas Coningsby was also a country gentleman.
He was a noted philanthropist, author, and member of Parliament.

At home, did little; walked over my ground, saw my oats ripe; took medicine to my ears. 2nd, was at the making up of my hay in Lanseague. . . . [3rd,] *Rain*: sent to Launceston for keeves [tubs] and wheels; began to make a say [assay] furnace [for testing metals mined on his property]. . . . A horse hurt Edward Cavell's son. 4th, *Vehement winds*: . . . Had some wheels and keeves from Launceston. 5th, great harm done to the corn [grain] by winds. Report that the manor of Colquite is set to sale. . . . 6th, began to malt my oats. . . . Met Mrs Coswarth riding to London and three of her sons. . . . 7th, *Great winds*: . . . Changed my calves' leas [pasture]. . . . [10th:] Rode to the Fair. . . . At this fair George Lower hurt William Courtenay. . . . [11th,] wrote and searched writings and evidences. 12th, Sunday, went to the church, met the new Vicar. 13th, *Showery*: wrote letters westward for money. Inch cut his corn at Dannonchapel. I looked on evidences. 14th, *Dark weather*: Matthew [Carnsew's younger son] rode westwards to do divers errands and to look for moneys. . . . 16th, *Rain*: to Roscarrock; it rained very much, yet rode thither. . . . 18th, sent J. Palmer to Port Eliot with gulls. Matthew came home and brought me moneys. . . . 19th, Sunday, communicated [took communion at church]. . . . A great swine died in the lust of eating poisoned rats, I think. . . . 21st, *Rain*: . . . My harvest folks wrought little or nothing, for wet weather, at home or at Dannonchapel; yet some of them took their wages. . . . 23rd, bound up my oats. . . . 24th, *St Bartholomew*: my wife and Jane Penkivell rode to Roscarrock. Variance [quarrel] between Thomas Roscarrock and Humphry Nicoll: much wind wasted between them. . . . Dreamed of mine elder brother. 25th, *Fair*: cut all my wheat at Dannonchapel, which is but sorry corn. Sent [the wheat] to the market. . . . 27th, began to carry [transport] corn. 28th, carried corn; some came from Dannonchapel. Reported that William Courtenay was dead. 29th, Calmady and his wife came to me, on wain [wagon] to Mr Butshed's to help in his corn. 30th, made my oats up [into sheaves]; cut all my beans and peas. 31st, rode to Bodmin to buy necessaries.

Rural Women

Good houswifely housewives, that let for no rest
Should eat when they list, and should drink of the best.
— THOMAS TUSSER, *A HUNDRETH GOOD POINTES OF HUSBANDRIE*

ALTHOUGH THE NATION WAS RULED BY A WOMAN, Elizabethan England was still a man's world. Women had few legal rights—for example, they could not sign contracts, make wills, or vote for representatives in town councils or Parliament. (As far as voting goes, though, it's worth remembering that most men could not vote, either, since the right was limited to well-off men with at least the rank of yeoman.) Legally, most women had the status of dependent children, always in the care of an adult male. Only widows whose fathers were dead were recognized as independent people by the law.

WIVES AND MOTHERS

A man was the absolute head of his household. Law, society, and religion all expected wives to be obedient to their husbands. At the same time, though, husbands were urged to treat their wives with

Opposite: Country women worked in the fields as well as in the home. This stained-glass image shows a woman harvesting wheat with her sickle, her face protected from the sun by a straw hat.

37

gentleness and care. For example, writer Nicholas Breton addressed the married man with this advice about his wife: "Cherish all good humors in her . . . force her to do nothing, rather prettily chide her from her labor, but in any wise commend [praise] what she doeth. . . . At table be merry to her, abroad [away from home] be kind to her, always be loving to her, and never be bitter to her."

Marital harmony was especially important in farm families, because most would not be able to thrive (or perhaps even survive) unless husband and wife worked together. The husband was the one who raised most of the crops and livestock, but it was the wife who was responsible for storing, budgeting, and preparing the family's supplies of food, clothing, and so on. As Thomas Tusser wrote:

Good husbands abroad, seeketh all well to have;
good housewives at home, seeketh all well to save.
Thus having and saving, in place where they meet,
make profit with pleasure, such couples to greet.

The division of labor described by Tusser extended from the common Elizabethan idea that, as another writer expressed it, "nature hath made [women] to keep home and to nourish their family and children." Indeed, since there were no reliable methods of family planning, most married women were either pregnant or looking after young children—often both—much of the time. Any other work they did had to allow them to also take care of their children. So women tended to stay in or close to the home, which was the safest and easiest place to tend to babies and toddlers. (When women did have to be away from the house, however, it was usually possible to have a servant, older daughter, relative, or neighbor look after the little ones for a while.)

USEFUL RECIPES

Although some recipe books were published in Elizabethan England, the average farmwife would not have owned one. If she knew how to write, though, she might record some of her favorite recipes, including ones she learned from friends and relatives. Whether written down or simply stored in her memory, her collection of recipes would contain not just foods but also a variety of home remedies and household hints. Here are a few examples:

TO STOP THE BLEEDING OF A WOUND
Take a piece of an old hat and burn it in the fire to a coal, then grind it to powder and straw [sprinkle] it into the wound.

TO MAKE A TART OF CHEESE
Take good fine paste [pastry dough] and drive it as thin as you can. Then take cheese, pare it, mince it, and bray [grind] it in a mortar with the yolks of Eggs till it be like paste, then put it in a fair dish with clarified butter, and then put it abroad into your paste and cover it with a fair cut cover [of pastry], and so bake it: that done, serve it forth.

HOW TO KEEPE FLYES FROM OILE PEECES
Pricke a Cowcumber [cucumber] full of barley cornes [grains] with the small spiring ends outward, make little holes in the Cowcumber first with a woodden or bone bodkin, and after put in the graine, these beeing thicke placed will in time cover all the Cowcumber, so as no man can discerne what strange plant the same should bee. Such Cowcumbers are to bee hung up in the middest of summer roomes to drawe all the flies unto them, which otherwise would flie upon the pictures or hangings.

A man and woman work together to prepare a meal in a well-equipped sixteenth-century kitchen.

Laundry day in the 1580s. The women must carry the laundry outside, scrub it, beat the dirt out of it, rinse it in the river, and hang it up or spread it out to dry in the sun.

HARD WORKERS

Women's work did not vary with the seasons as much as men's did. Every day there were the meals to prepare and the children to look after. Keeping the house clean was a continuous job, and laundry day came every Saturday. There was always spinning, weaving, sewing, mending, or knitting to be done. Housewives made thread, sheets, towels, tablecloths, shirts, caps, stockings, and other items—and not just for family use, but often for sale. Another item that women could produce both for the family and to sell was ale. When a housewife had brewed a large batch, she might hang a bushy green plant on a pole outside the door to let the community know she had ale for sale, and for as long as it lasted, her home would become a public alehouse.

A farmwife's labors started even before breakfast. She had to build up the fire, milk the cow, strain the milk, get the children up and dressed, pack a lunch for her husband to take to the fields (if he wasn't planning to come back to the house to eat), and prepare breakfast for the family and servants. This was usually an easy meal, often just porridge or bread and butter; no one could linger over breakfast when there was so much work to get to. The housewife also had to feed the poultry and pigs in the morning. And in springtime the chickens would start laying, so she would need to gather their eggs early each day.

Then she had to prepare lunch (usually referred to as dinner),

40

which was the main meal for the average family. It was served around noon, or a bit earlier. A typical menu in a well-off household might be stew or soup, boiled or roasted meat, vegetables or a salad, cheese and nuts, and fruit or a bread pudding for dessert. Pies were also very popular, filled with meat or fruit. Poorer people might just have a bowl of stew, made mostly with boiled grains and vegetables, and would usually have to get their protein from what the Elizabethans called "white meat," meaning eggs and dairy products. But prosperous or poor, no one had time for a sit-down meal in the house during haymaking and harvest. Instead people ate in the fields, making a quick lunch of bread and butter, cheese, and hand-sized pies.

Supper, eaten between 6:00 and 9:00 p.m., was a simple meal, often leftovers, so the farmwife could spend her afternoon on other tasks. She might take grain to the local mill to be ground into flour. She could make bread, ale, cheese, butter, or herbal medicines. Her

Most women spent a great deal of time spinning. They sometimes set up their spinning wheels outdoors so that they could enjoy the fresh air and the comings and goings of their neighbors.

Young women were often hired as farm laborers, especially during harvesttime.

afternoon could be devoted to preserving food for the winter (she always had to be planning ahead): drying herbs, beans, peas, fruits, and fish; salting butter and meats; pickling vegetables and seafood; making fruit preserves. It was no surprise if she sometimes felt overwhelmed by everything she had to do. One sixteenth-century book advised the housewife, "It may fortune sometime that thou shalt have so many things to do that thou shalt not well know where is best to begin. Then take heed which thing should be the greatest loss if it were not done and in what space it would be done; and then think what is the greatest loss, and there begin."

Another responsibility was the kitchen garden. The farmwife began working it in March, when she planted seeds for herbs and vegetables. During this month she would also plant plots of flax and hemp. Then all spring and summer she had to weed around her plants, protect them from pests, and keep them growing strong. She picked the herbs as she needed them and the vegetables as they came ripe. In July she could harvest her hemp and flax; then there were several steps in processing the plants to make them ready for spinning into fiber. During the busy agricultural seasons, she was likely to be in the fields making hay and harvesting. It was especially common for women to follow the harvesters and bind the cut grain into sheaves and then to winnow the grain after threshing. Women also knew how to use scythes and sickles, and they could stack hay and load carts as necessary, too.

As we have seen, though, the fieldwork was normally done by men. So while the husband was out tending his crops, it was the wife's job to take produce, eggs, cheeses, and poultry to town to sell on market day, and there she could also buy things that her family needed. For those who lived not too far from London, there were even more marketing opportunities, as writer John Norden noted in 1593:

> These [farmers] commonly are so furnished with kine [cows] that the wife twice or thrice a week conveyeth to London milk, butter, cheese, apples, pears, frumenty [wheat boiled in milk], hens, chickens, eggs, bacon and a thousand other country drugs [products], which good housewives can frame and find to get a penny. And this yieldeth them a large comfort and relief.

All this goes to show what an important role women played in rural life and in the economy of the nation. Women worked long, hard hours for the good of their families and communities—as Thomas Tusser knew well:

> Though husbandry seemeth to bring in the gains,
> Yet huswifery labours seem equal in pains.
> Some respite to husbands the weather may send,
> But housewives' affairs have never an end.

Family and Children

Those that do teach young babes
Do it with gentle means and easy tasks.
—Shakespeare, *Othello*

ALMOST EVERYONE IN ELIZABETHAN ENGLAND EXPECTED to marry and have children. Most people, though, waited till they were at least in their mid to late twenties to get married. They were generally free to choose their own spouses, but parents and even influential neighbors were likely to take a hand in arranging matches, especially if the families were wealthy and important. Love, or being in love, was not given much consideration. It was more important that the couple like and respect each other so that they could live and work together as friends and companions. Since getting a divorce was nearly impossible, mutual compatibility seemed the best guarantee that a marriage would be a lifelong successful partnership.

COMING INTO THE WORLD

Soon after marriage, a woman would begin to look for signs that

Opposite: This section of a painted wooden panel shows a mother and her newborn son being visited by her women friends. All the family's finest serving pieces are displayed on the table for the occasion.

45

she was pregnant. Both men and women anticipated becoming parents. But many also feared the process, because a lot could go wrong during pregnancy. Miscarriages and other complications were common. Childbirth was even more dangerous, especially since medical knowledge and techniques were much more limited than today. A large number of mothers and babies died during or soon after birth.

Once a woman knew she was expecting, she did what she could to ensure her and her baby's survival. She could get assistance from the local midwife, a respectable woman with much experience in caring for women and delivering babies. The midwife would examine her periodically and prescribe herbal medicines that might help with having a healthy pregnancy. Probably she would also pass along the common advice that pregnant women should avoid all extremes—in the weather, in their food, in their activities, in their emotions. It was believed that any kind of shock, even a sudden loud noise, could be harmful. Husbands were urged to take extra care to protect their expectant wives from such things.

Along with trying to follow the midwife's advice, many mothers-to-be took communion more often at church and prayed special prayers. Often their husbands did, too. There was also a wide variety of folk practices thought to help pregnant women, such as wearing a special belt or an "eagle stone," a small stone within a slightly larger one. One midwife in the 1600s wrote, "I have proved it to be true, that this stone hanged about a woman's neck and so as to touch her skin, when she is with child, will preserve her safe [during the pregnancy] . . . and will cause her to be safe delivered when the time comes."

When it was time for the birth, clean white sheets were put on the bed, the windows were curtained over, the fire was built up to keep the room warm, and the husband sent for his wife's married

women friends. These women and the midwife helped the mother through the birth, but the father was not allowed to be present. The women provided care and encouragement, and helped distract the mother from her pain by telling jokes and funny stories. If everything went well and mother and baby lived, the women celebrated with a feast right there in the birth room. Then they would visit almost every day while the mother was recovering from the birth. Bringing a baby into the world in Elizabethan England was an important social event for a community's women.

Immediately after birth, the midwife washed the baby, wrapped it in linen bands called swaddling, and let the father see his newborn child. Then she brought the baby back to the mother, who nursed it for the first time. If the mother did not survive, however, a wet-nurse would have to be found—perhaps a neighbor who was nursing a

A touching family portrait from the 1630s illustrates a situation that was also common during Elizabeth's time. The father sadly bids farewell to his dead first wife, the mother of his two little girls, but also looks forward to the future happiness promised by his second wife, who holds their newborn child on her lap.

baby of her own. If this was not possible, a baby bottle could be made out of a cow's horn, and the baby could be given cow's or sheep's milk. Most children were breast-fed for about two years.

Newborns were treated very tenderly. They slept in a cradle in the same room as their parents, or sometimes in the same bed. A mother could keep her infant close, even while she was working outdoors, by carrying it in a cloth sling. When the baby cried for no obvious reason, parents would rock it or walk up and down with it, jiggling it in

ELIZABETHAN NURSERY RHYMES

Like parents today, Elizabethan parents entertained their young children and helped them learn language with songs and nursery rhymes, such as

> Pillycock, pillycock, sat on a hill,
> If he's not gone—he sits there still.

A number of nursery rhymes still known today probably date back to Elizabethan times (or even earlier), for example, "Who Killed Cock Robin," "Little Jack Horner," "Thirty Days Hath September," and "Mary Mary Quite Contrary." Some people think that the following rhyme commemorates a visit by Queen Elizabeth to the market town of Banbury:

> Ride a cockhorse* to Banbury Cross   [*rocking horse]
> To see a fine lady upon a white horse.
> Rings on her fingers and bells on her toes,
> She shall have music wherever she goes.

a soothing way, as described in this lullaby by John Phillip:

What creature now living would hasten thy woe?
Sing lullaby, lullaby, lullaby baby:
See for thy relieving, the time I bestow
To dance and to prance thee, as prett'ly as may be.

GROWING UP

Country children probably had a variety of homemade toys. We can easily imagine a father spending some winter evenings carving wooden animals, for example, and a mother sewing up scraps of cloth to make rag dolls. Other toys included wooden tops and balls made of leather or of tight-wound rags. An inflated pig's bladder functioned as a kind of balloon, and animal bones could be used as pieces in a game like jacks. The rural environment offered a variety of playthings, such as flowers to make daisy chains and beautiful but short-lived dolls, leaves and twigs to make boats to float on ponds and streams, and stones and clay to make mud pies, miniature buildings, and more. Imagination gave children many possibilities: a stick, for example, could be a scepter or a sword or a horse. Some children in well-to-do families had hobbyhorses, rocking horses, or similar fancy toys.

Two-year-old Lady Arabella Stuart with a doll—both dressed in the same elaborate style worn by wealthy Elizabethan women

Rural children did not have much time to devote to play. Around the age of six, some would start going to school, usually in the local market town, where they would learn to read and perhaps to write and do basic arithmetic. Most of these students stayed in school for only a few years; after that they needed

A merchant's wife, recently identified by scholars as Alice Barnham, helping her two sons learn to read and write. Both of them grew up to become wealthy country gentlemen.

to work to help their families. Yeomen and gentlemen, though, usually sent their sons on to grammar school to learn Latin, Greek, history, and philosophy. After that, many of these boys would finish their education at Oxford or Cambridge, England's two universities, or in London at the Inns of Court, which functioned as law schools. Some boys were taught at home, at least part of the time, by tutors or by their own fathers. Gentleman-farmer William Carnsew, for example, noted in his diary several Latin books that he read with his sons. Girls were nearly always educated at home, with most of the focus on household skills.

Children in the countryside generally started helping around the house and farm soon after they could walk. Young children were able to do such chores as scattering feed for chickens, pulling weeds in the kitchen garden, and scaring birds away from the growing crops. Boys learned to use a bow and arrow for this purpose and might spend all day on guard in the fields, as Thomas Tusser described:

Then forth with thy slings, and thine arrows and bows:
till ridges be green, keep the corn from the crows.
A good boy abroad, by the daystar appear,
shall scare goodman crow, that he dare not come near.

As children grew, getting stronger and more skilled, they took greater part in adult work. Girls worked alongside their mothers at spinning, sewing, laundry, cleaning, making soap and candles, and so on. Boys herded cattle, sowed crops, plowed fields, drove pigs into the woods to eat acorns in autumn, and in general assisted their fathers. Both girls and boys pitched in at harvest, gathering up the grain and binding it into sheaves, carrying food and drink out to the harvesters, or helping in other ways.

As teenagers, many girls and boys left their families to work as servants or laborers for someone else, usually a relative or prominent neighbor. This gave them the chance to earn money that they might save toward marrying and having their own household. Even young people who were well provided for often went to live with another family, which could give them more educational and social opportunities than they might have at home. Numerous country teenagers, though, felt that the best opportunities of all lay in the cities, especially London. Unfortunately, most who left the countryside found that they had just exchanged one set of hardships for another—few people in Elizabethan England had a completely easy life, no matter where they lived.

Country Pleasures

Although they take pains on the working days,
yet they may go leap, shoot, dance, dice, card, and bowl,
and use what gaming they shall think good on the Sunday and holiday.
—John Fit John, *A Diamonde Most Precious . . .*

COUNTRY PEOPLE WORKED VERY HARD, BUT EVEN IN the midst of their labors they often managed to enjoy themselves. If they were working together in the fields, they would naturally chat and joke with one another. During haymaking and harvest, young women and men found time to flirt, and everyone enjoyed relaxing with their friends during meal breaks. Market days and fairs offered many opportunities for socializing and catching up on news, as well as for shopping and possibly seeing jugglers and other entertainers.

William Carnsew's diary records his visits to numerous people as he tended to his landholdings. After business was done, they might dine together and then play a game. The games mentioned by Carnsew include card games, lawn bowling, quoits (like horseshoes), tables (similar to backgammon), and shovegroat (which involved pushing a metal disc across a table). Carnsew and his

Opposite: Music, dancing, and feasting make this wedding celebration in a village south of London a festive occasion for the entire community.

friends often gambled on these games, and when Carnsew won he usually mentioned it in his diary, sometimes recording the exact amount of his winnings. In any case, he seems to have been good at finding time for recreation even as he went about the business of running his farms.

SPORTS AND PASTIMES

Sports were very popular; then as now, they were favorite activities on Sunday afternoons and holidays. The Elizabethans even had a form of football—like soccer, but much rougher and with larger teams. It was typically played in the streets and could involve all the men of the village. Another favorite men's sport was bandy ball, which was very similar to modern field hockey. An ancestor of base-ball and cricket called stoolball was played by both men and women.

Other sports or active games included archery, footraces, variants of tag, swimming, wrestling, and throwing heavy stones to see who could hurl them the farthest. Country people also enjoyed fishing and hunting—and if they were successful, they'd be able to bring home protein-rich food for the family. It was important, though, only to hunt where you were allowed—poaching, taking game from someone else's land, was a serious offense.

Another much-loved recreation was dancing, generally in groups rather than couples. Typically everyone held hands and danced in a circle or in a long line; some dances involved leaping or stomping. Music was provided by bagpipes or by pipe and tabor (a pennywhistle-like instrument and small drum, played at the same time by one person). People liked to sing, too, especially rounds—which the Elizabethans called catches—and ballads. A ballad was a

These men are playing an early form of golf, which became increasingly popular in England during the sixteenth century.

Country Pleasures

55

long rhyming song that told a story. Sometimes it was a tale about people from history or legend, such as King Arthur or Robin Hood. Other ballads told love stories or funny stories or stories about fairies. Still others related or commented on current events—everything from sensational murders to the deeds of English soldiers fighting in the war against Spain.

Ballads were often printed on a single sheet of paper called a broadside, which people could buy from a ballad seller at a fair or market. Although the majority of country dwellers were illiterate, most villages had at least a few residents who could read. They would learn the words to a new ballad (which were always set to a popular tune) and then teach it to others, perhaps when they were all relaxing together in an alehouse at the end of the day. The literate could also read other things for people—for instance, personal letters, government proclamations, and selections from the Bible or a popular book (though only the well-off would be likely to own any books).

Storytelling was a favorite way to pass the evenings, especially in the winter. Then people sat indoors knitting, spinning, making baskets, mending tools, and doing similar tasks, and could easily entertain one another with stories as they worked. Shakespeare refers to this often in his plays, as in these lines from *Richard II*:

In winter's tedious nights, sit by the fire
With good old folks, and let them tell thee tales
Of woeful ages long ago betid.

Portrayed on a tapestry, a man returns from a successful hunting trip. Hunting was a favorite rural pastime, both as a form of recreation and a way of putting food on the table.

Shakespeare in fact titled one of his later plays *The Winter's Tale*, and in it a character remarks on the type of story people most enjoyed during this season: "A sad tale's best for winter. I have one / Of sprites and goblins."

Country people would have nodded in recognition at this. And some of them did have the opportunity to see Shakespeare's plays. His acting company, like others, sometimes left London to tour other parts of England. They visited not just the larger cities but market towns, too, where people eagerly came from the surrounding countryside to see them perform. Toward the end of his life, a man born in the same year as Shakespeare recalled the excitement of such an occasion when he was a boy: "My father took me with him and made me stand between his legs, as he sat upon one of the benches, where we saw and heard very well. . . . This sight took such impression in me, that when I came towards man's estate, it was as fresh in my memory as if I had seen it newly acted."

Local people sometimes put on plays as part of village fairs and festivals, and sometimes professional acting companies visited country towns, often performing on a temporary stage in the yard of an inn.

CELEBRATING THE SEASONS

Most people worked six days a week and took Sunday as a day of rest and (after the morning church service) recreation. They also observed a number of holidays through the year. Nearly all were religious, but they usually had nonreligious aspects, too—as with holidays today, celebrations took a variety of forms. In addition, country dwellers preserved many old festive traditions that recognized the turning points in the agricultural year.

Spring was greeted with special joy. "The fields breathe sweet, the daisies kiss our feet, / Young lovers meet, old wives a-sunning sit," wrote poet Thomas Nashe, and:

> Spring, the sweet spring, is the year's pleasant king;
> Then blooms each thing, then maids dance in a ring,
> Cold doth not sting, the pretty birds do sing:
> *Cuckoo, jug-jug, pu-we, to-witta-woo!*

Easter was observed mainly with church services and family dinners. Two weeks later, though, came Hock Tuesday, the first of the year's warm-weather festivities. On this day in many parts of England, women would go out and wait for men to come by and then capture them with a rope and demand a "ransom" payment. They donated the money they received to the local fund to help the poor.

For the Elizabethans, the first of May marked the arrival of summer. May Day celebrations were merry and sometimes chaotic. Many people got up very early in the morning and went out to the woods and meadows to gather greenery and flowers, especially birch branches and hawthorn blossoms, which they brought back to deck their windows and doorways. They would also fetch a tree trunk to serve as their maypole; it was hauled from the woods by a

Villagers gather around their maypole for dancing, feasting, and general merrymaking.

team of oxen with flowers on their horns, followed by a crowd of laughing and singing men, women, and children. Then, according to writer Philip Stubbes,

> This Maypole . . . is covered all over with flowers and herbs, bound round about with strings, from the top to the bottom, and sometime painted with variable colours. . . . And thus being reared up with handkerchiefs and flags hovering on the top, they strew the ground round about, bind green boughs about it, set up summer halls, bowers and arbors hard by it. And then fall they to dance about it.

The dancing went on not just for the rest of that day (and night), but all through the summer, on Sundays and in the evenings. The leaders of the festivities were often a group of morris dancers, men who dressed in green or yellow or some other light color and danced with handkerchiefs in their hands and bells tied around

their legs. A few of the morris dancers were costumed: as a woman (called Maid Marian), a horse (the Hobbyhorse), a jester (the Fool), and sometimes as other characters. Philip Stubbes—who did not approve of such things—described the merriment this way:

Then march these heathen company towards the church and churchyard, their pipers piping, their drummers thundering, their stumps dancing, their bells jingling, their handkerchiefs swinging about their heads like madmen, their hobbyhorses and other monsters skirmishing amongst the rout [crowd]. And in this sort they go . . . into the church (though the minister be at prayer or preaching) dancing and swinging their handkerchiefs over their heads. . . . Then the foolish people they look, they stare, they laugh, they fleer [snicker], and mount upon forms [benches] and pews to see these goodly pageants.

The revelers ended up in the churchyard—often the best place in a village to hold an outdoor gathering—where, according to Stubbes,

The Countryside

they feasted and danced the rest of the day and sometimes all night.

Such festivities provided country people with a welcome release from their daily work and worries. Soon enough they would be absorbed by the hard labor of bringing in the harvest. But the completion of the harvest was, not surprisingly, the occasion for another great celebration, called harvest home. Paul Hentzner got this glimpse of one community's harvest home as he traveled through the English countryside:

> Their last load of corn [grain] they crown with flowers, having besides an image richly dressed, by which, perhaps, they would signify Ceres [the Roman goddess of grain]; this they keep moving about, while men and women, men and maid servants, riding through the streets in the cart, shout as loud as they can till they arrive at the barn.

Once the grain was safely stored away, it was time for a feast, with all the singing and dancing and high spirits appropriate to the occasion.

Christmas brought another period of revelry, and women welcomed it by decorating the home with green ivy and holly. Like Easter, the day itself was generally one for church, prayer, and family. But December 26 began the twelve days of Christmas, during which people visited friends and relatives, feasted, sang carols, played games, exchanged gifts, and generally enjoyed themselves. As Thomas Tusser described the season:

> Beef, mutton and pork, shred pies of the best,
>   pig, veal, goose and capon, and turkey well drest;
> Cheese, apples and nuts, jolly carols to hear,
>   as then in the country is counted good cheer.

7

Hard Times

Fair Summer droops, droop men and beasts therefore;
So fair a summer look for never more.
All good things vanish, less than in a day,
Peace, plenty, pleasure, suddenly decay.
— Thomas Nashe, *Summer's Last Will and Testament*

PEOPLE IN ELIZABETHAN ENGLAND, WHETHER THEY lived at court, in the city, or in the country, faced many of the same challenges. Foremost among these was disease. Limited sanitation and medical techniques meant that illness was common, spread easily, and often could not be cured. Women and babies still die in childbirth today, but not in the numbers they did in the sixteenth century. And conditions that are now considered not very serious, or easily preventable or treatable, killed a great many people then— diarrhea and measles, for example. People who lived in boggy areas were at high risk for malaria, carried by mosquitoes that thrived in those moist conditions. There were also a number of epidemics of smallpox and black plague, frightening diseases that could seriously disfigure or kill.

Although the Elizabethans didn't know about germs, they did

Opposite: A dying man is surrounded by his family, his minister, his lawyer, and his doctor. Although this scene was painted some years after Elizabethan times, medical practice hadn't changed much: the doctor makes his diagnosis by examining a flask of the patient's urine.

understand that many illnesses spread from person to person through the air. They also realized that crowding made epidemics worse, and they had some idea that buildups of sewage and garbage in public areas (such as streets and gutters) created unhealthy conditions. For these reasons, almost everyone agreed that the country was more wholesome than the city. In addition, upper-class people, such as those involved in the intrigues of the court or the details of "big business," looked to the country as a place to relax and get away from their cares. Poets contrasted the "falseness" and ambition of court and city life with the "naturalness" and honest labor of country life, as in this song from Shakespeare's *As You Like It* (sung by a nobleman living in the Forest of Arden):

> Who doth ambition shun,
> > And loves to live i'th' sun,
> > Seeking the food he eats
> > And pleased with what he gets,
> Come hither, come hither, come hither.
> > Here shall he see
> > No enemy
> But winter and rough weather.

BAD WEATHER, BAD HARVESTS

Of course, country life was nowhere near as carefree as poets portrayed it. For farmers, "rough weather" was no small matter. True, the English climate was generally mild enough that apricots, figs, and grapes could be grown, at least in some parts of the south. In this region snow was rare, although several winters were so cold that the Thames River froze over and people could walk across it. And rain was generally plentiful—but sometimes too much so, for

rain at the wrong time could ruin the crops. Shakespeare knew this very well, and in *A Midsummer Night's Dream* describes the results of a season of "contagious fogs" and flooding rivers:

The Thames frozen over, the ice so thick that people could set up tents and hold a winter fair

> The ox hath therefore stretched his yoke in vain,
> The ploughman lost his sweat, and the green corn
> Hath rotted ere his youth attained a beard.
> The fold stands empty in the drownèd field,
> And crows are fatted with the murrain flock.

For most of Elizabeth's reign, harvests were good. But there were three years in the 1580s and four or five in the 1590s when the crops failed. The harvests of the 1590s were especially bad, and thousands of poor people starved—in the country because they did not have grain to eat or sell, and in the city because they could not afford to buy what grain or bread was available, for the prices were high.

The Romance of the Countryside

In a literary tradition that went back to ancient Greece and Rome, Elizabethan poets often wrote about an idealized country life, with carefree shepherds and shepherdesses spending their days in singing and romance. This type of poetry is called pastoral, from Latin *pastor*, "shepherd." One of the most popular Elizabethan pastoral poems was and still is Christopher Marlowe's "The Passionate Shepherd to His Love":

Come live with me and be my love,
And we will all the pleasures prove
That valleys, groves, hills, and fields,
Woods, or steepy mountain yields.

And we will sit upon the rocks,
Seeing the shepherds feed their flocks,
By shallow rivers to whose falls
Melodious birds sing madrigals.

And I will make thee beds of roses
And a thousand fragrant posies,
A cap of flowers, and a kirtle
Embroidered all with leaves of myrtle;

A gown made of the finest wool
Which from our pretty lambs we pull;
Fair linèd slippers for the cold,
With buckles of the purest gold;

A belt of straw and ivy buds,
With coral clasps and amber studs:
And if these pleasures may thee move,
Come live with me, and be my love.

The shepherd swains shall dance and sing
For thy delight each May morning:
If these delights thy mind may move,
Then live with me and be my love.

Marlowe's poem was so popular that Shakespeare quoted it, and Sir Walter Raleigh even wrote the shepherdess's response:

If all the world and love were young,
And truth in every shepherd's tongue,
These pretty pleasures might me move
To live with thee and be thy love.

Time drives the flocks from field to fold
When rivers rage and rocks grow cold,
And Philomel becometh dumb;
The rest complains of cares to come.

The flowers do fade, and wanton fields
To wayward winter reckoning yields;
A honey tongue, a heart of gall,
Is fancy's spring, but sorrow's fall.

Thy gowns, thy shoes, thy beds of roses,
Thy cap, thy kirtle, and thy posies
Soon break, soon wither, soon forgotten—
In folly ripe, in reason rotten.

Thy belt of straw and ivy buds,
The coral clasps and amber studs,
All these in me no means can move
To come to thee and be thy love.

But could youth last and love still breed,
Had joys no date nor age no need,
Then these delights my mind might move
To live with thee and be thy love.

A flood in Wales in the early 1600s drowned not only fields but whole villages.

These were especially hard times for farmers who rented the land they worked. If they could not produce a crop, they could not pay their rent and they would lose their farm. Even in a good year, many families found it difficult to meet their expenses. And tenants frequently owed their landlords other fees and fines as well. For example, William Carnsew noted several occasions in his diary when he collected a farm animal from the family of a dead tenant. This was a kind of "death tax" called a heriot, and it was one of the traditional payments that tenants owed to the lord of the manor.

The situation was even more difficult for farmworkers hired to work land owned or rented by others. They got to enjoy little, if any, of the produce they raised, as Edward de Vere, the Earl of Oxford, wrote:

The Countryside

The labouring man, that tills the fertile soil
And reaps the harvest fruit, hath not in deed
The gain, but pain; and if for all his toil
He gets the straw, the lord will have the seed.

If these laborers had a cottage and a bit of land, they could grow some vegetables and keep some animals of their own. But they might not be able to eat their eggs or chickens or the fruit from their trees—sometimes selling them was the only way to get money for other needs.

"ENCROACHING UPON THE POOR"

Earlier, we saw that many people believed that farming "in several" was a more productive form of agriculture than open-field farming. Throughout the sixteenth century, more and more champion country was being converted to individual farms. This could happen when one farmer was able to buy up adjacent strips in the common fields or when a large landowner simply decided that he wanted his property farmed in several. Either way, the huge fields would be broken up and the new farms enclosed by hedges or stone walls. This process was called enclosure, and it was practiced on an even larger scale when landowners decided to convert their lands to sheep pastures—in many areas, wool was more profitable than grain, and raising sheep required fewer laborers than raising crops.

Enclosure made the rich richer, but it could cause tremendous hardship for people at the lower end of the scale. Some authors tried to draw attention to the plight of these people. In 1590, for example, Charles Gibbon wrote, "Is there not such amongst us as do enlarge their own livings by encroaching upon the poor, by eating up their lands, in buying houses over their heads, by abridging

A man arrested for stealing a purse makes the best of his punishment in the stocks, and a friend even brings him a mug of ale.

their liberties, and taking away their commons?" In spite of such calls to conscience, numerous poor people continued to lose their homes and livelihoods—all the more tragic because families of cottagers and tenant farmers often had rented the same property for generations. Many of the dispossessed went to the cities to look for work; others wandered the roads as beggars. Social welfare systems were only just being set up, so homeless laborers had few sources of help and few options open to them. They must have felt like the hungry, exiled character in Shakespeare's *As You Like It* who asked,

> What, wouldst thou have me go and beg my food,
> Or with a base and boisterous sword enforce
> A thievish living on the common road?
> This I must do, or know not what to do.

And yet the dream of an ideal rural life lived on, as did many rural communities. The values of those communities survived, too—values such as cooperation, generosity, and honesty. Perhaps the epitaph of country gentleman Robert Trencreek best sums up the ideal:

A lover of his country, friendly to his neighbours, liberal to the poor; . . . his ready advice . . . and bountiful hospitality to all did manifest a man of a constant resolution in the carriage of his life.

GLOSSARY

apprentice a young person being trained in a craft or trade by assisting and working for a master in that craft or trade

bodkin a slender dagger or a tool used for punching holes, especially in cloth

chaff husks and other unwanted plant material that must be separated from harvested grain

champion or **champaign** (related to French *champ*, "field") level, open country; also refers to the open-field agriculture that was traditionally practiced in such country

fallow unplanted. Letting a field lie fallow for a season or more gave the soil a chance to "rest" and replenish its nutrients.

husbandry agriculture. The Elizabethans used the word *husband* to mean a farmer as well as to mean a married man.

madrigal a song for a small number of unaccompanied singers, each singing a different melody

Parliament the legislative branch of the English government, made up of the House of Commons and the House of Lords. In Elizabeth's time, it only met when the monarch summoned it, and its main function was to approve taxes and major changes in policy.

peat ancient decayed and compressed vegetation found in boggy areas; dug up, cut into blocks, and dried, it can be burned as fuel

rushlight a light made from a dried rush (a kind of marsh grass) soaked in grease; it was held in place by an iron clip

FOR FURTHER READING

Ashby, Ruth. *Elizabethan England.* New York: Benchmark Books, 1999.

Crompton, Samuel Willard. *Queen Elizabeth and England's Golden Age.* Philadelphia: Chelsea House, 2005.

Greenblatt, Miriam. *Elizabeth I and Tudor England.* New York: Benchmark Books, 2002.

Hinds, Kathryn. *Life in the Renaissance: The Countryside.* New York: Benchmark Books, 2004.

Lace, William W. *Elizabethan England.* San Diego: Lucent Books, 2005.

Weatherly, Myra, ed. *Living in Elizabethan England.* San Diego: Greenhaven Press, 2004.

ONLINE INFORMATION*

Best, Michael. *Shakespeare's Life and Times.*
   http://ise.uvic.ca/Library/SLT/intro/introsubj.html

Encyclopedia Britannica. *Guide to Shakespeare.*
   http://www.britannica.com/shakespeare

Jokinen, Anniina. *16th Century Renaissance English Literature (1485–1603).*
   http://www.luminarium.org/renlit

Renaissance: The Elizabethan World.
   http://elizabethan.org

Shakespeare Resource Center.
   http://www.bardweb.net

*All Internet sites were available and accurate when this book was sent to press.

SELECTED BIBLIOGRAPHY

Ault, Norman, ed. *Elizabethan Lyrics from the Original Texts.* 3rd ed. New York: William Sloane Associates, 1949.

Barber, C. L. *Shakespeare's Festive Comedy: A Study of Dramatic Form and Its Relation to Social Custom.* Cleveland: World Publishing Company, 1963.

Clarke, Amanda. *Growing Up in Elizabethan Times*. London: B. T. Batsford, 1980.

Cressy, David. *Birth, Marriage and Death: Ritual, Religion, and the Life-Cycle in Tudor and Stuart England*. Oxford: Oxford University Press, 1997.

Editors of Time-Life Books. *What Life Was Like in the Realm of Elizabeth: England AD 1533–1603*. Alexandria, VA: Time-Life Books, 1998.

Greenblatt, Stephen. *Will in the World: How Shakespeare Became Shakespeare*. New York: W. W. Norton, 2004.

Hentzner, Paul. *Itinerarium Angliae (1612), with a translation by Robert Bentley, and annotations by Horace Walpole*. Hypertext edition by Dana F. Sutton, 2004. http://www.philological.bham.ac.uk/hentzner

Kelsey, Harry. *Sir Francis Drake: The Queen's Pirate*. New Haven: Yale University Press, 1998.

Logan, George M., et al., eds. *The Norton Anthology of English Literature*. Vol. 1B, *The Sixteenth Century, The Early Seventeenth Century*. 7th ed. New York: W. W. Norton, 2000.

Orlin, Lena Cowen. *Elizabethan Households: An Anthology*. Washington, DC: The Folger Shakespeare Library, 1995.

Pritchard, R. E., ed. *Shakespeare's England: Life in Elizabethan and Jacobean Times*. Stroud, Gloucestershire: Sutton Publishing, 1999.

Reed, Michael. *The Age of Exuberance, 1550–1700*. London: Routledge & Kegan Paul, 1986.

Rowse, A. L. *Court and Country: Studies in Tudor Social History*. Athens: University of Georgia Press, 1987.

Rowse, A. L. *The England of Elizabeth: The Structure of Society*. Madison: University of Wisconsin Press, 1978.

Shapiro, James. *A Year in the Life of William Shakespeare: 1599*. New York: HarperCollins, 2005.

Singman, Jeffrey L. *Daily Life in Elizabethan England*. Westport, CT: Greenwood Press, 1995.

Tusser, Thomas. *A hundreth good pointes of husbandrie*. E-text transcribed by Risa Bear from the Dobell edition of 1909. University of Oregon, 2003. http://darkwing.uoregon.edu/~rbear/tusser1.html

Weatherly, Myra, ed. *Living in Elizabethan England*. San Diego: Greenhaven Press, 2004.

SOURCES FOR QUOTATIONS

This series of books tries to bring the people of Elizabethan England to life by quoting their own words whenever possible. When necessary for clarity, however, we have modernized the Elizabethan spellings preserved in the sources. All Shakespeare quotations are from William Shakespeare, *Complete Works, Compact Edition,* edited by Stanley Wells et al. (Oxford: Clarendon Press, 1988).

Chapter 1

p. 9 "There fruitful corn": Edmund Spenser, *Colin Clouts Come Home Againe,* available online at http://darkwing.uoregon.edu/%7Erbear/colin.html (spelling modernized).

p. 9 "This land of such": Shakespeare, *Richard II,* act 2, scene 1.

p. 10 "There are many hills": Hentzner, *Itinerarium Angliae.*

p. 12 "Good land that is": Rowse, *The England of Elizabeth,* p. 95.

p. 12 "Our soil being divided": Pritchard, *Shakespeare's England,* p. 53.

p. 14 "And how like you": Shakespeare, *As You Like It,* act 3, scene 2.

p. 16 "Yeomen are those": Pritchard, *Shakespeare's England,* p. 11.

Chapter 2

p. 19 "Thy houses and barns": Tusser, *A hundreth good pointes of husbandrie* (spelling modernized).

p. 20 "have neither dairy": Weatherly, *Living in Elizabethan England,* p. 18.

p. 21 "Flowers to smell": Ault, *Elizabethan Lyrics,* p. 184.

p. 22 "of old time" and "But as horn": Orlin, *Elizabethan Households,* p. 7.

p. 25 "Many farmers": ibid., p. 84.

Chapter 3

p. 27 "A man may behold": Rowse, *The England of Elizabeth,* p. 72.

p. 30 "Thy servant": Tusser, *A hundreth good pointes of husbandrie* (spelling and punctuation modernized).

p. 32 "I am shepherd": Shakespeare, *As You Like It,* act 2, scene 4.

p. 33 "they are good": Hentzner, *Itinerarium Angliae.*

p. 35 "At home, did little": Rowse, *Court and Country,* pp. 160–163.

Chapter 4

p. 37 "Good housewifely housewives": Tusser, *A hundreth good pointes of husbandrie* (spelling and punctuation modernized).

p. 38 "Cherish all good": Singman, *Daily Life in Elizabethan England,* p. 18.

p. 38 "Good husbands": Tusser, *A hundreth good pointes of husbandrie* (spelling and punctuation modernized).

p. 38 "nature hath made": Singman, *Daily Life in Elizabethan England,* p. 18.

p. 39 "To stop the bleeding": Orlin, *Elizabethan Households,* p. 104.

p. 39 "To make a Tart": *A Book of Cookrye,* available online at http://jducoeur.org/Cookbook/Cookrye.html (spelling modernized).

p. 39 "How to keepe flyes": Editors of Time-Life Books, *What Life Was Like in the Realm of Elizabeth,* p. 89.

p. 42 "It may fortune": Pritchard, *Shakespeare's England,* p. 70.

p. 43 "These [farmers] commonly are": Rowse, *The England of Elizabeth,* p. 72.

p. 43 "Though husbandry seemeth": Pritchard, *Shakespeare's England,* p. 51.

Chapter 5

p. 45 "Those that do teach": Shakespeare, *Othello,* act 4, scene 2.

p. 46 "I have proved": Cressy, *Birth, Marriage and Death,* p. 24.

p. 48 "Pillycock": Greenblatt, *Will in the World,* p. 23.

p. 49 "What creature": Ault, *Elizabethan Lyrics,* p. 41.

p. 51 "Then forth with thy": Tusser, *A hundreth good pointes of husbandrie* (spelling and punctuation modernized).

Chapter 6

p. 53 "Although they take pains": Orlin, *Elizabethan Households,* p. 47. (The full title of the quoted source is *A Diamonde Most Precious, Worthy to be Marked: Instructing all Maysters and Servauntes, How They Ought to Leade Their Lyves.*)

p. 56 "In winter's tedious": Shakespeare, *Richard II,* act 5, scene 1.

p. 57 "A sad tale's best": Shakespeare, *The Winter's Tale,* act 2, scene 1.

p. 57 "My father took": Greenblatt, *Will in the World,* p. 30.

p. 58 "The fields breathe" and "Spring, the sweet": Ault, *Elizabethan Lyrics,* p. 164.

p. 59 "This Maypole": Barber, *Shakespeare's Festive Comedy,* pp. 21–22.

p. 60 "Then march these heathen": ibid., p. 28.

p. 61 "Their last load": Hentzner, *Itinerarium Angliae*.

p. 61 "Beef, mutton and pork": Rowse, *The England of Elizabeth*, p. 93.

Chapter 7

p. 63 "Fair Summer droops": Barber, *Shakespeare's Festive Comedy*, p. 60.

p. 64 "Who doth ambition": Shakespeare, *As You Like It*, act 2, scene 5.

p. 65 "contagious fogs" and "The ox hath": Shakespeare, *A Midsummer Night's Dream*, act 2, scene 1.

p. 67 "If all the world": ibid., p. 879.

p. 67 "Come live with me": Logan, *The Norton Anthology of English Literature*, pp. 989–990.

p. 69 "The labouring man": Ault, *Elizabethan Lyrics*, p. 74.

p. 69 "Is there not": Orlin, *Elizabethan Households*, p. 75.

p. 70 "What, wouldst thou": Shakespeare, *As You Like It*, act 2, scene 3.

p. 71 "A lover of his country": Rowse, *Court and Country*, p. 146.

INDEX

ABOUT THE AUTHOR

 KATHRYN HINDS grew up near Rochester, NY. In college she studied music and writing, and went on to do graduate work in comparative literature and medieval studies. She has written more than twenty-five books for young people, including the books in the series LIFE IN ANCIENT EGYPT, LIFE IN THE ROMAN EMPIRE, LIFE IN THE RENAISSANCE, and LIFE IN THE MIDDLE AGES. Kathryn lives in the north Georgia mountains with her husband, their son, and an assortment of cats and dogs. When she is not reading or writing, she enjoys spending time with her family and friends, dancing, knitting, gardening, and taking walks in the woods. Visit her online at www.kathrynhinds.com

Fox Gradin, Celestial Studios Photography